Chapter 4
Changes in Ecosystems

You Will Discover

- how living things depend on each other and their environment.
- how living things interact in an ecosystem.
- how ecosystems change.
- how changes to the environment affect living things.

pearsonsuccessnet.com

Build Background

How do changes in ecosystems affect our world?

competition

succession

hazardous waste

Chapter 4 Vocabulary

competition page 114

parasite page 117

host page 117

succession page 118

extinct page 120

endangered page 120

hazardous waste page 126

parasite

host

extinct

endangered

Lab zone: Directed Inquiry

Explore What is the effect of crowding on plants?

Materials

small paper cups

pencil

spoon

potting soil

90 radish seeds

water

Process Skills

By **observing** the plants as they grow, you **collect data** which show the effects caused by crowding plants.

What to Do

1. Use a pencil to make 4 small holes in the bottom of each cup. Half fill each cup with potting soil.

2. Sprinkle 10 radish seeds in one cup. Sprinkle 80 seeds in the other cup. Cover the seeds in both cups with potting soil.

3. Add 5 spoonfuls of water to both cups. Put them in a bright place. Add 1 spoonful of water to both cups daily.

4. Every few days for 3 weeks **collect data** about the radish plants in each cup. **Observe** carefully. Record their number and appearance.

Label the cups.

Explain Your Results

Based on your **observations**, which cup has healthier plants after 3 weeks? Explain.

How to Read Science

 **Cause and Effect**

A **cause** is why something happens. An **effect** is what happens. Sometimes clue words such as *because* and *since* signal a cause and effect. Sometimes there are no clue words or the author does not tell why something happened. The student who wrote the lab report below **observed** the effects of having too many plants growing close together.

Lab Report

Procedure

Day	Procedure	Observations
1	We planted radish seeds in two small milk cartons. We filled each milk carton with garden soil. We planted 3 radish seeds in carton A and 100 radish seeds in carton B.	The cartons are the same size and contain the same amount of soil. The only difference is the number of seeds.
7	We watered the seeds in each carton every two days.	The seeds are beginning to grow. We can see a few plants in carton A. We see more plants in carton B.
20	The plants have been growing for two weeks.	The plants in carton A are very tall and full. The plants in carton B are much smaller and look crowded.

Apply It!

Make a graphic organizer like the one at the right. Use it to explain the **observations** of what happened to the carton with more seeds.

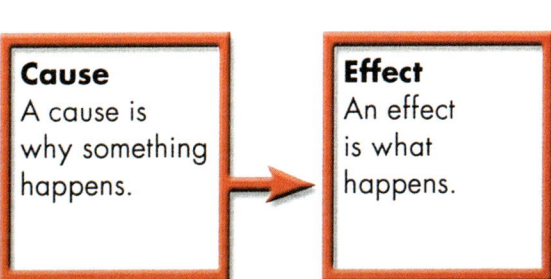

You Are There!

A chipmunk pops out of its burrow and scampers across the forest floor. You hold your breath and stand very still. The chipmunk stops and touches a mushroom that is only a few feet from you. The interaction between the chipmunk and the mushroom is one of many interactions in the ecosystem. With so many interactions taking place, how does the ecosystem stay balanced?

Lesson 1

How are ecosystems balanced?

All living things depend on one another and their environment to live and grow. Interactions among living and nonliving things help maintain balance in ecosystems.

Needs of Living Things

The Eastern American chipmunk is just one of more than 10,000 animal and plant species that live in the Great Smoky Mountains.

Each day, the chipmunk depends on the living and nonliving things in the forest to survive. It gets food from the fungi and plants that grow in the forest environment. The plants also provide oxygen, which the chipmunk needs to breathe. It drinks rainwater that collects in nearby puddles and streams. It digs its burrow in the rocky ground near the base of a tree. The burrow protects the chipmunk from cold weather and predators, such as hawks and foxes.

All plants and animals need food, water, living space, shelter, light, and air to grow and be healthy. Each kind of organism also needs the right soil and weather conditions. Living things get what they need from the environment in which they live. Living things can survive only in environments where their needs are met.

The forests of the Great Smoky Mountains meet all the needs of the Eastern American chipmunk.

1. **Checkpoint** What do all plants and animals need to live and grow?
2. **Writing in Science Expository** In your **science journal,** write about an ecosystem near your school. List at least two plants and two animals in that ecosystem. Identify three things each plant and animal needs.

111

A Balancing Act

Ecosystems are healthy when all their parts are in balance. All the living things in an ecosystem are interrelated, so what happens to one population affects the entire community.

In a way, balancing an ecosystem is like balancing a seesaw. Suppose one side of the seesaw holds the food supply, living space, and shelter for a group of animals. If the number of animals that the food and space will support is on the other side, the seesaw is in balance. If more animals were to get on, there would not be enough food or room to go around. The animal side of the seesaw would drop, and the seesaw would no longer be balanced.

The seesaw example is also true for plants. They need water, sunlight, and minerals from the soil. Plants also need space. Many seedlings might sprout from tree seeds that are planted close together. But many of the seedlings will not become trees because they do not have enough living space.

All organisms help keep the balance of an ecosystem. For example, rabbits eat grasses. Rabbits help keep grass from taking over the space that other plants might need. Red foxes eat rabbits. The foxes help keep the rabbit population from getting too large and eating all the grass. The grass and other plants provide oxygen and moisture that the animals need.

Balanced ecosystems are always changing. Organisms are born. They live, die, and then decompose. Change helps keep ecosystems in balance. Some changes cancel each other out. For example, water evaporates from a pond, but water is replaced when it rains. Animals use oxygen, but plants make oxygen as part of the process of photosynthesis.

Populations of these animals use the resources of the Great Smoky Mountains.

✓ Lesson Checkpoint

1. What happens when the number of organisms in a population increases?
2. What are two things that might prevent a plant population from growing in size?
3. **Math in Science** Suppose 40 foxes live in a forest community. If hunters capture $\frac{1}{5}$ of the fox population, how many foxes would be captured?

Lesson 2

How do organisms interact?

Organisms in an ecosystem compete for and share resources. They have other relationships too.

Change in Ecosystems

Populations in ecosystems change naturally as the amount of resources changes. Think about the chipmunk at the beginning of the chapter. A population of chipmunks will grow where food is plentiful. As the population increases, more food, more water, and more living space are needed. Eventually, the population may use up these resources.

Then, as resources decrease, each chipmunk will have less food to eat, less water to drink, and less space in which to live. Some chipmunks will die or move out of the area. As the population decreases, more resources will be available for the remaining chipmunks. The population begins to grow, and the cycle starts again.

Competing

Populations grow when their needs are met. But populations that share an ecosystem may need the same resources. When two or more species must use the same limited resources, **competition** occurs. Every organism has adaptations that help it compete for resources. An organism that competes successfully is more likely to survive and reproduce.

Living space is one cause of competition. Plant species compete for light and water. Bird species compete for the same nesting site. Predators compete for prey.

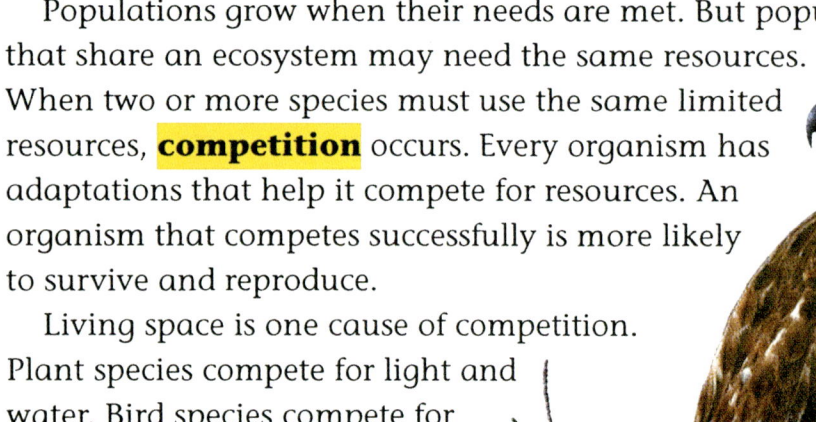

Sharing Resources

Certain behaviors help animals avoid or reduce competition. For example, both owls and hawks feed on some of the same animals. Because hawks hunt during the daytime and owls hunt at night, competition is reduced.

Living in groups can make it easier to obtain food or stay protected. Wolves are predators that usually hunt large herbivores, such as deer. Several wolves will work together to hunt a deer. Deer protect themselves from wolves by traveling in groups. With many deer bunched together, it is hard for a pack of wolves to attack any individual deer.

1. **✓Checkpoint** What are two behaviors that help animals avoid or reduce competition?
2. **Cause and Effect** Identify the cause and effect of deer traveling in groups.

Living Side by Side

Two different organisms can live closely together for most or all of their lives. This relationship may be helpful to both organisms, or it may help one organism but not the other. These special relationships exist between animals, plants, fungi, protists, and bacteria.

Moss and oak trees, as shown in the picture, live together. The tree provides the moss with a sheltered living space, but the moss does not help or harm the oak tree.

Some animals also have this kind of relationship. Beetles, silverfish, and other insects sometimes travel with army ants. They eat whatever food is left as the ants march along. They have no effect on the army ants.

Helping Each Other

Lichens are two organisms that help each other. Lichens are combinations of fungi and algae that live together, often on the surface of rocks. The algae supply the fungi with sugar, nutrients, and water. The fungi protect the algae from too much sunlight and very warm temperatures. Neither organism could survive in its habitat without the other.

Lichens often grow on rocks or the bark of trees.

Mistletoe is a parasite plant that takes water and nutrients from its host tree.

Causing Harm

Sometimes a close relationship between two organisms helps one but harms the other. The organism that is helped is called a **parasite.** Parasites are organisms that live on or in another organism. The organism that is harmed by the parasite is called the **host.** Both plants and animals can act as parasites and as hosts. A parasite uses its host as a source of food.

An insect called the balsam woolly adelgid is a parasite that kills Fraser fir trees of the Appalachian Mountains. As the insects feed, they harm the trees.

The larvae of the Asian long-horned beetle burrow deep into a tree, eventually killing the tree.

Lesson Checkpoint

1. What is a parasite?
2. What might happen to the parasite if its host were to die?
3. **Social Studies in Science** Use a map to locate the Appalachian Mountain system. In which states are the Appalachians found?

Lesson 3

How do environments change?

Environments naturally change over time. These changes can occur very slowly or very quickly. Changes to an environment can affect ecosystems and the species that inhabit them.

The Process of Change

Thousands of years ago, a forest may have been a lake filled with fish and water plants. Over many years, the lake dried up and was replaced by a marsh. And later still, trees began to grow, replacing the marsh grasses and bushes.

This process of gradual change from one community of organisms to another is called **succession.** Succession occurs as the environment changes. Changes in an environment affect the communities within it. As communities change, conditions might change also. New conditions allow different communities to grow.

At first, the newly formed lake has no living things. In time, rivers carry soil into the lake. Algae, bacteria, and spores from fungi are in the soil.

The algae and other organisms add nutrients to the lake. The lake can now support small plants. Insects that eat the plants enter the ecosystem. Herbivores also become part of this new community.

One Step at a Time

In most cases, succession occurs in stages. If conditions are right, bare land might become grassland. Grassland will give way to shrubs. Shrub land will become a forest. Communities grow and replace one another until there is a stable community with few changes.

Changes in climate may also affect ecosystems. Climate is the average temperature, winds, and rainfall for an area over many years. Climates change very slowly over a long period of time. More than 15,000 years ago, snow and ice covered parts of North America. Trees, grasses, and many flowering plants could not grow. As the climate became warmer, plants and animals moved in. Eventually the plants and animals formed the forest communities we see today.

1. **Checkpoint** What is succession?
2. **Art in Science** Draw pictures or make models of the stages of succession described in the first paragraph of this lesson.

Birds, insects, reptiles, fish, and mammals live and interact in the lake community. As time passes, the lake slowly fills with soil, fallen leaves, and material from decomposed organisms. The lake gradually changes into a marsh.

After many years, the marsh has filled with sediments. It dries up. Pine, oak, and hickory trees begin to grow. The marsh has gradually changed into a forest community.

Changing Species

In the 1800s, people watched huge flocks of passenger pigeons fly over the Great Smoky Mountains. By 1915, not a single passenger pigeon was alive. These birds had become **extinct.** The entire species was gone forever.

A species will become extinct if the species does not change as Earth changes. Climate changes, volcanoes, and even meteors may cause extinction. Human activities also may cause extinction. Habitat destruction and hunting are big problems for some species.

Once a population drops below a certain number, the species may not be able to recover. Populations of some species have been reduced so much that they are in danger of becoming extinct. These species are called **endangered** species. Species that may soon become endangered are threatened species. Both endangered and threatened species sometimes leave an area to search for better habitats.

Hunting, poisoning, and habitat destruction caused red wolves to become extinct in the wild during the 1980s. Red wolves bred in captivity are slowly being returned to their natural communities.

Habitat destruction and hunting killed the passenger pigeon.

In 1970, the peregrine falcon was an endangered species. People worked hard to save the species. By 1999, it was no longer endangered.

Species Then and Now

Fossils show us that life on Earth has not always been the same. Over long periods of time, changes in the environment have caused species to change. Scientists can compare fossils of things that lived long ago with things that are alive today.

Woolly mammoths lived long ago. They have since become extinct, but some mammoths remain as fossils. Some have been frozen solid. Scientists compare these frozen mammoths with modern elephants. Both have large tusks and long noses. Their bones are also very much alike. Both the mammoths and the modern elephants are classified in the same family.

Fossils can also tell us about the environment long ago. Sometimes fossils of marine creatures are found on land in dry climates. These fossils tell scientists that long ago shallow seas must have covered the area where the fossils were found.

1. **Checkpoint** When are species considered threatened?
2. **Cause and Effect** Why do organisms become extinct?

In ancient times, many kinds of sea lilies filled the oceans. Many sea lilies have been preserved as fossils.

Today only a few species of sea lilies remain. These flower-like animals attach themselves to the ocean floor.

121

Rapid Changes

A hurricane's strong winds rip up trees and flatten plants. Heavy rains and huge waves flood a coastal community. Lightning strikes a tree, starting a forest fire that burns almost everything in its path.

Hurricanes, floods, and fires, along with volcanic eruptions and earthquakes, are natural events that can quickly change the landscape. These rapid changes may force species to leave the area because the resources they need are no longer available.

Before the Fire
Fire can spread quickly with fuel from dead branches, dry leaves, and rotting plants. During periods with little rain, a fire can spread even faster.

Although some rapid events are destructive, they also play an important part in keeping an ecosystem balanced. Fires help clear away dead and dying plant matter, making more room for new plants to grow. Some trees, such as the Table Mountain pine, have sealed cones that open when they come in contact with the heat of a fire. The ash from a volcanic eruption enriches the soil.

Natural Disasters

In the spring and summer of 1993, huge amounts of rain caused the Mississippi and Missouri Rivers to overflow. Some areas were flooded for almost 200 days. The floods left thousands of acres of land covered with sand and mud.

The floods affected many plants and animals. Grasses and trees died because of too much water. Birds had fewer offspring because many nesting places were destroyed. But the populations of some fish increased. They used the flooded areas to feed and reproduce.

Forest Ablaze
Lightning and human carelessness can start forest fires. The temperature of a forest fire can reach 700°C.

After the Fire
Forest fires leave only the charred remains of trees and brush. They destroy many habitats. But they clear land, and very quickly new plants begin to grow.

✓ Lesson Checkpoint

1. Name two processes that change an environment over a very long period of time.
2. What are two events that change an environment very quickly?
3. **Writing in Science** **Descriptive** Suppose that you live for 75 years in the same location. Write a paragraph in your **science journal** describing how the environment might change during your lifetime.

Lesson 4

How do people disturb the balance?

Human activities change environments. When ecosystems change, some organisms die or leave the area. Other organisms adapt to the changes and survive.

People and the Environment

Like all organisms, humans interact with their environment. We get our food, shelter, and water from the land and organisms that surround us. Unlike other organisms, we can change large parts of the environment to meet our needs. We cut down trees to provide us with lumber and land for houses. We clear prairies to plant crops or build roads. When we change the environment, however, we sometimes upset the balance of ecosystems.

We also affect ecosystems with wastes from the products we make and use. These waste products can pollute the air we breathe and the water we drink. Many of the things we do release dust, dirt, and harmful gases into the air. Automobiles and factories can release harmful chemicals into the air. These chemicals can harm plants. Animals that depend on these plants may lose their source of food or shelter.

Natural Air Pollution Detector

Lichens grow just about everywhere—in soil, on tree trunks and branches, on rocks, roofs, and walls. These organisms are sensitive to the air pollutant known as sulfur dioxide. The air surrounding some cities is so polluted that lichens cannot survive. Whether or not lichens can grow is one indicator of the air pollution in an area.

Polluted Water

Water becomes polluted when wastes and chemicals get into rivers, lakes, and oceans. Some of these substances enter the water through sewer systems. Other chemicals are used on land to help plants grow or to kill insects. Rain washes these chemicals off the land and into the water. Some of these chemicals can harm or kill fish and other plants and animals that live in or near the water.

Some of the pollutants in rivers and streams may end up in Earth's oceans. Oil is a pollutant that can harm the ocean's plants and animals. Sometimes, spills and leaks occur during the drilling and shipping of oil. Algae, plants, mollusks, and fish become coated with oil and die. Birds that are coated with oil often drown.

Fire on the Water

In 1952, the Cuyahoga River caught fire. The river was heavily polluted with oil, logs, and other wastes. The fire burned because of the oil floating on the water. A fire on the river in 1969 led to the Clean Water Act, which made it illegal for anyone to put pollutants into water.

1. **Checkpoint** Why do humans have a great impact on the environment?
2. **Technology in Science** When an oil spill occurs, members of the International Bird and Rescue Research Center (IBRRC) carefully wash any oil-soaked birds with a dishwashing liquid. Research other processes that are used to help animals survive oil spills.

Land Pollution

Garbage, litter, and other substances can pollute the land. Humans produce huge amounts of garbage. Every day, each person throws away about 2 kilograms of garbage. Most of this trash is dumped into landfills and then covered with soil.

Disposing of hazardous wastes can cause other kinds of land pollution. **Hazardous wastes** are substances that are very harmful to humans and other organisms. These substances may be poisonous, cause disease, start fires, or react dangerously with other substances. Until recently, most hazardous wastes were put into containers and buried in the ground. Some of these containers leaked. The hazardous wastes seeped into the ground or water and damaged nearby habitats.

Stripping Away the Land

Many valuable substances lie under Earth's surface. One of these substances is coal. Strip mining has been one way to get coal that is below Earth's surface. At one time, huge machines dug up and cleared away the top layers of soil. Large holes were left. The land surrounding the holes began to erode. Piles of soil and rock were washed into ponds and rivers. The nearby ecosystems were greatly affected.

Restoring the land is important for the environment. Habitats are restored, and animals can return to the area. If this restoration is not possible, crops are planted so that the land is useful.

This huge machine is used to dig for coal.

Birds and other animals may look for food in a landfill.

Land Reclamation

Federal law requires that land disturbed by mining must be reclaimed. Reclaiming means that mining companies must replace rock and soil that were removed. They must replant the area with crops or native trees and grasses. Mining companies must submit a plan to reclaim the land they use before the first shovel ever touches the ground.

Coal mining in some states began in the 1840s. For more than 100 years, no repairs were made to lands that had been strip-mined. Then, beginning in the 1970s, laws were passed to regulate strip-mining. For example, the Surface Mining Control and Reclamation Act law requires that coal companies study the ecosystems before any digging begins. The companies then must plan how to restore the land after they finish mining.

California is one state that has reclaimed some mining areas. An area in Sacramento County where gravel was dug has now been restored to its natural water habitat. Other areas grow alfalfa, corn, and other crops. A field of strawberries now covers one mining area.

A young tree is being protected as it grows.

1. **Checkpoint** What human activities damage the environment?
2. **Art in Science** Make a brochure or poster that tells about ways to reduce different types of pollution.

Preserving the Environment

Our nation has many natural treasures. You can watch millions of gallons of water cascade over Niagara Falls or look out over the breath-taking Grand Canyon. The United States has established the National Parks system to preserve nature's beauty, historic sights, and the habitats of many plants and animals.

Yellowstone National Park
In 1872, Yellowstone became the world's first national park. Most of the park is in Wyoming. Many kinds of trees and other plants and animals, such as bears and moose, live there. Yellowstone's most unusual features are bubbling mud pots and geysers that shoot boiling water high into the air.

Saguaro National Park
Saguaro National Park is in the Sonoran Desert in Arizona. The Sonoran Desert is home to more species of plants and animals than any other American desert. It is the only region in the world where giant saguaro cactuses grow. This monument preserves ancient villages as well as modern wildlife.

Okefenokee National Wildlife Refuge
This refuge in Georgia is the home of many plants and animals. Cranes, herons, egrets, and other waterfowl wade in the marshy areas. Bobcats, deer, otters, and other animals roam in the grassy areas. They are protected from poachers, people who hunt without a license. Decaying vegetation sometimes makes the water in the Okefenokee brown.

Everglades National Park
Everglades National Park in Florida is a subtropical area. It is a refuge for the wildlife that lives in wet habitats. The park is only a portion of the area called the Everglades. Big Cypress Swamp and many islands off the coast are also in the Everglades.

Lesson Checkpoint

1. What are some of the effects of habitat destruction?
2. What are some things people have done to protect the environment?
3. **Social Studies in Science** On the Internet or at the library, find out more about how the National Park system was started. Write about what you find in your **science journal.**

Lab zone Guided Inquiry

Investigate How can a change in the environment affect plant growth?

Changing conditions can affect which plants can grow in a place. In some farming areas, irrigation has led to a buildup of salt in the soil. This can affect which plants are able to grow there.

Materials

paper cups

pencil

plastic spoon

potting soil

30 radish seeds

tap water

salty solution

very salty solution

Process Skills

When you record information you have **observed**, you are **collecting data**.

What to Do

1) Use a pencil to make 3 small holes in the bottom of each cup. Use a spoon to fill the cups $\frac{2}{3}$ full of potting soil.

2) Place 10 radish seeds on top of the potting soil in each cup. Add a thin layer of potting soil.

Label the cups.

3) Add 5 spoonfuls of water to each cup. Use tap water in cup A, salty water in cup B, and very salty water in cup C. Every day put 1 spoonful of water into each cup.

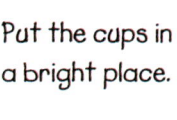

Put the cups in a bright place.

4. **Observe** the cups every day for 10 days.

5. **Collect data.** Every day record how many radish plants are in each cup.

	Effect of Salt on Radish Plants		
Day	Number of Radish Plants		
	Cup A (tap water)	Cup B (salty water)	Cup C (very salty water)
Day 1			
Day 2			
Day 3			
Day 4			

Explain Your Results

1. How did salt in the environment change how radish plants grew?
2. **Infer** How might a buildup of salt in the soil affect a farmer?

Go Further

Are there plants that can grow in salty soils? Make a plan to investigate this or other questions you may have.

Math in Science

Recycling a Fraction

Since 1990, Americans have thrown out about 2 kg of garbage per day for every person in the country. That's about 56 kg per week for a family of 4! This garbage doesn't just disappear. Most of it is buried in landfills, some of it is burned, and a fraction of it is recycled. The pictures below show how this fraction has changed, as recycling has become more popular with Americans.

 Recycled

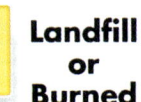 Landfill or Burned

What fraction of the garbage was recycled in 1990?

The picture for 1990 shows 6 equal parts.

One part represents the recycled garbage.

$$\frac{1}{6}$$ ← One part is recycled
← Six equal parts in all

In 1990, $\frac{1}{6}$ of the garbage was recycled.

1990   1995   2000

Use the pictures on page 132 to answer the questions.

1. In 1995, what fraction of the garbage was recycled?
   A. $\frac{1}{4}$
   B. $\frac{1}{3}$
   C. $\frac{1}{2}$
   D. $\frac{3}{4}$

2. In 1995, what fraction of the garbage was put into landfills or burned?
   F. $\frac{1}{4}$
   G. $\frac{1}{3}$
   H. $\frac{1}{2}$
   I. $\frac{3}{4}$

3. In 2000, what fraction of the garbage was recycled?
   A. $\frac{7}{10}$
   B. $\frac{3}{10}$
   C. $\frac{1}{3}$
   D. $\frac{1}{7}$

4. In 2000, what fraction of the garbage was put into landfills or burned?
   F. $\frac{7}{10}$
   G. $\frac{3}{7}$
   H. $\frac{3}{10}$
   I. $\frac{7}{3}$

5. About how much garbage (in kg) does a family of 8 throw out each day? In 1995, how much of this garbage (in kg) was recycled? Remember: $\frac{1}{4}$ of $n = n \div 4$

Lab zone Take-Home Activity

Find out how much garbage your family would throw out in a day, in a week, and in a year at the rate of 2 kg per person per day. Find how many kilograms of garbage would be recycled in one year if your family recycled $\frac{1}{10}$ of the garbage they throw out.

Chapter 4 Review and Test Prep

Use Vocabulary

competition (p. 114)	**hazardous waste** (p. 126)
endangered (p. 120)	**host** (p. 117)
	parasite (p. 117)
extinct (p. 120)	**succession** (p. 118)

Use the vocabulary term from the list above that completes each sentence.

1. An organism that feeds on and harms a living thing is called a(n) _____.

2. A species that is _____ has no living members.

3. _____ is the struggle between organisms to meet their needs.

4. A species that is at risk of dying out is a(n) _____ species.

5. _____ can be very harmful to organisms and the environment.

6. The process of one community gradually replacing another community is _____.

7. A(n) _____ is an organism that provides energy or an environment for another organism.

Explain Concepts

8. Animals carry away seeds that stick to their fur. Explain how this relationship helps one organism but does not help or harm the other.

9. Suppose an ant colony lives on a tree. What is the effect of chopping down the tree?

10. In 2003, the list of endangered species included 82 fish, 20 amphibians, 78 reptiles, 258 birds, and 316 mammals. About how many times as great was the number of endangered species of mammals as that of reptiles?

Process Skills

11. **Infer** Suppose you find the fossil skull of an animal with sharp teeth like those of a wolf. What might you infer about what this animal ate?

12. **Observe** What observations could you make that would help you determine that living things in an area interact with other living things?

13. **Predict** A tree in a forest was struck by lightning, causing a large fire. The grasses, bushes, and trees in the forest all burned. Predict how the ecosystem will change.

Cause and Effect

14. Make a graphic organizer like the one shown below. Fill in two more possible causes of the effect that is described.

Causes

1. Number of predators increases.
2.
3.

Effect

Rabbit population decreases in number.

 Test Prep

Choose the letter that best completes the statement or answers the question.

15. A pet-store gerbil has lived alone in a cage. Suppose you were to put it in a cage with two other gerbils. How can the pet-store gerbil survive in its new environment?
- Ⓐ It must wait to eat until the other gerbils have finished.
- Ⓑ It must build a new home.
- Ⓒ It must compete with the other gerbils for resources.
- Ⓓ It must hide in the cage.

16. One result of two different species living in the same area and using the same limited resources is
- Ⓕ succession.
- Ⓖ learned behavior.
- Ⓗ pollution.
- Ⓘ competition.

17. Nonliving things that affect organisms in an ecosystem include soil, temperature, and
- Ⓐ plants.
- Ⓑ water.
- Ⓒ decomposers.
- Ⓓ parasites.

18. Suppose you found a rock that had imprints of water plants and shells. What does this tell you about the area in which you found the rock?
- Ⓕ It was once under water.
- Ⓖ It was once a forest.
- Ⓗ Dinosaurs once lived there.
- Ⓘ Many predators lived there.

19. Explain why the answer you chose for Question 15 is best. For each answer you did not choose, give a reason why it is not the best choice.

20. **Writing in Science** **Expository** Explain how predators and parasites are different and alike.

Career Ecologist

Ecologists explore the world of living things and how they interact with the environment. Ecologists are scientists who help us understand the connections between an organism and everything around it. They work in many environments—cities, suburbs, forests, farms, freshwater habitats, and oceans.

Ecologists do different jobs for different organizations. Sometimes they work indoors, and sometimes they work outdoors. Parks, nature centers, wildlife refuges, government research labs, museums, zoos, aquariums, conservation organizations, and field stations are some of the places where ecologists study living things. NASA's Kennedy Space Center includes Merritt Island National Wildlife Refuge. More than 200 species of birds and several endangered species live there. NASA ecologists work to protect the ecosystems from activities associated with space shuttle and rocket launches.

People with different training work as ecologists. They are high school or college graduates. Some have even more education. They all like being outdoors and exploring the world around them. They all are curious about how the environment works and how it changes.

Rebecca Bolt Smith is a wildlife ecologist at NASA. Her work at the Space Center provides information about ecosystems on Earth.

Lab zone Take-Home Activity

Many clubs have ecology programs. Some communities also have ecology activities in parks. Look in your local library or on the Internet to find an ecology activity that you and your friends can do in your community.